An Educator's Guide to
Teacher Reflection

Barbara Larrivee
California State University

James M. Cooper, Series Editor
University of Virginia

HOUGHTON MIFFLIN COMPANY   BOSTON   NEW YORK

Senior Sponsoring Editor: Sue Pulvermacher-Alt
Senior Development Editor: Lisa Mafrici
Editorial Assistant: Dayna Pell
Manufacturing Coordinator: Chuck Dutton
Marketing Manager: Jane Potter

Copyright © 2006 Houghton Mifflin Company. All rights reserved.

No part of this work may be reproduced or transmitted in any form or by any means, electronic or mechanical, including photocopying and recording, or by any information storage or retrieval system without the prior written permission of Houghton Mifflin Company unless such copying is expressly permitted by federal copyright law. Address inquiries to College Permissions, Houghton Mifflin Company, 222 Berkeley Street, Boston, MA 02116-3764.

Printed in the U.S.A.

ISBN: 0-618-57285-6

456789-VHO-10 09 08

CONTENTS

Preface	vi
Part I: Introduction	1
Part II: Knowledge	5
Defining Reflective Practice	5
Attributes and Attitudes of Reflective Practitioners	7
Key Elements of Reflective Practice	8
Levels of Reflection	12
Reflection Direction	20
4-Step Process for Guiding Reflection	22
Part III: Applications	23
The Capacity To Reframe: A Crucial Attribute of Reflective Practitioners	23
Avenues to Developing Reflective Practice	24
Action Research	30
Part IV: Extensions	32
For Reflection	33
Glossary	34
References	37

PREFACE

Houghton Mifflin Company publishes outstanding education textbooks in the areas of foundations of education, introduction to education, educational psychology special education, and early childhood education. These textbooks introduce students to many concepts, policies, and research that undergird educational practice. However, as is the case for virtually all introductory texts, many topics are introduced but not covered in great depth. The Houghton Mifflin Teacher Education Guide Series is designed to provide more in-depth coverage of selected educational topics studied in the teacher education curriculum.

At the present time, there are seven guides in the series:

- Classroom Management
- Field-based Classroom Observation
- Diversity in the Classroom
- Classroom Assessment
- Inclusion
- Technology Tools
- School-based Intervention Programs
- Student Motivation
- Teacher Reflection
- Differentiating Instruction

The topics for these guides were selected because they are addressed in virtually all teacher education programs, and contain vital information for beginning teachers if they are to be successful in the classroom. Instructors may use the guides either for required or enrichment reading.

Each of these guides provides pre-service teachers with greater in-depth knowledge, application suggestions, and additional resources on its particular topic. All the guides share a common format that includes an introduction to the topic, knowledge that the prospective teacher should possess about the topic, examples of and suggestions for how the knowledge can be applied, and resources for further exploration. Each guide also contains 10-15 questions designed to help the prospective teacher reflect on the concepts and ideas introduced in the guide, as well as a glossary of key terms.

Some teachers stagnate after a few years of teaching, falling into ruts and routines, while other teachers grow and continue to develop professionally over the course of their careers. A primary explanation for this phenomenon is the concept of teacher reflection. As Barbara Larrivee explains in this guide, teachers who develop the habit and skills of reflective practice are more effective in meeting student needs, in developing a more complex understanding of teaching issues, and in growing continuously as a professional teacher.

PART I: INTRODUCTION

WHY TEACHERS NEED TO BE REFLECTIVE PRACTITIONERS

There are many reasons for teachers to develop as reflective practitioners. Perhaps the most important is that teachers need to be reflective in order to deal with the inevitable uncertainties and tradeoffs involved in everyday decisions that affect the lives of students. Given all the complexities, ambiguities, and dilemmas that characterize today's classrooms, effective teachers will need to engage in both critical inquiry and thoughtful reflection, the hallmarks of reflective practitioners. Teaching is a complex and dilemma-ridden endeavor, necessitating ongoing learning as well as the capacity to be reflective. Many view the development of reflective practice as the foundation for the highest professional competence (Cole & Knowles, 2000; Jay, 2003; Larrivee, 2000; Osterman & Kottkamp, 2004; Steffy, Wolfe, Pasch, & Enz, 2000; Valli, 1997; York-Barr, Sommers, Ghere & Montie, 2001; Zeichner & Liston, 1996).

Because today's classroom represents increasing diversity among students, a teacher has to accommodate and adjust to this greater range of differences in ethnicity, socioeconomic status, developmental levels, motivation to learn, and achievement. Being responsive to this vast array of students' needs requires teachers who are reflective. Engaging in reflection helps teachers recognize behaviors and practices which impede their potential for tolerance and acceptance-the vital elements for meeting the needs of all students in a diverse society moving toward a global community.

Growing demands on teachers with recently imposed federal and state mandates often lead to a sense of alienation and isolation leaving teachers feeling like mere pawns in the system. However, teachers really can influence their practice much more than they may think by engaging in systematic reflection about their work. By taking control of their teaching lives they become empowered decision makers who can then begin to act on their world in a way that can change it. Reflective practitioners come to see themselves as change agents, capable of understanding not only what is, but also working to create what could be.

Another reason for developing as reflective practitioners is that it frees teachers from routine and impulsive acts, enabling them to act in a more deliberative and intentional manner. While following routine helps teachers manage the task of teaching, if teachers become slaves to routine they eventually come to feel powerless to influence their future careers. When teaching becomes so habitual that it is tantamount to a mechanical act it can be the path to burnout. Routine action is guided by circumstance, tradition and external authority (Zeichner & Liston, 1987). On the other hand, reflective practice entails voluntarily and willingly taking responsibility for considering personal actions.

A final reason is that emerging beliefs about quality teaching support teachers developing as reflective practitioners. What constitutes quality teaching is evolving. Major curricular changes that provide greater emphasis on curricular integration, teaching for meaning, interactive dialogue, socialization, and collaboration require fundamental changes in the way teachers view their role. These changing classroom demands redefine the teacher's role as social mediator, learning facilitator, and reflective practitioner (Larrivee, 2000). Being able to function in these roles begins with teacher self-awareness, self-inquiry and self-reflection. In fulfilling these roles, teachers in turn help students to learn to exercise self-direction, self-regulation and self-reflection – those qualities that are fundamental for democratic citizens.

This shift is characterized by a move from teacher-directed lessons to more participatory learning, from teacher solicitation of specific student responses to interactive dialogue, and from the teacher questioning students to students generating their own questions. Accordingly, the teacher role shifts from deliberately controlling learning to facilitating learning. The student role shifts from passive recipient of teacher-directed instruction to interactive participant, often functioning in a variety of collaborative modes with peers. This transformation is guided by the assumption that students construct their own meaning and take responsibility for their own learning.

REFLECTION IS A VITAL TOOL FOR NAVIGATING LIFE IN TODAY'S CLASSROOM

The explicit goal of reflective practice is to create deeper understanding and insight, forming the basis for not only considering alternatives, but also for taking action to continually improve practice throughout one's teaching career. Becoming a reflective practitioner means perpetually growing and expanding, opening up to a greater range of possible choices and responses to classroom situations. Building the habit of reflective practice allows teachers to remain fluid in the dynamic environment of the classroom.

Reflective practitioners operate in a perpetual learning spiral in which dilemmas surface, constantly initiating a new cycle of planning, acting, observing, reflecting, and adapting.

HISTORICAL PERSPECTIVE

John Dewey (1910/1933, 1938) is generally credited with the foundational influence on reflection in education. He made the distinction between action that is routine and action that is reflective, contrasting reflective thinking with habits of thought that are unsystematic, lack evidence, rely on mistaken beliefs or assumptions, or mindlessly conform to tradition and authority. Although Dewey first proposed his ideas nearly a century ago, the spirit of the concept remains essentially the same.

In the early 1980s, the notion of reflective practice in the United States was popularized primarily based on the work of Schön. Schön's (1983, 1987) work criticized the then reigning portrayal of teacher as technician. He challenged the belief system of teacher as technician, replacing it instead with teacher as committed and autonomous decision maker, or reflective practitioner. According to Schön, reflective practitioners continually learn from their experience, reconstructing experience through reflection.

The term reflection characterizes a way of thinking that accepts uncertainty and acknowledges dilemmas, (e.g., Dewey, 1933, 1938; Kelsey, 1993; King & Kitchener, 1994; Sparks-Langer & Colton, 1991; Osterman & Kottkamp, 2004). In his writings, Dewey asserted that the capacity to reflect is initiated only after recognition of a problem or dilemma *and* the acceptance of uncertainty. The dissonance created in understanding that a problem exists engages the reflective thinker to become an *active inquirer*, involved in both the critique of current conclusions and in the generation of new hypotheses. According to Dewey, reflective thinking requires continual evaluation of beliefs, assumptions and hypotheses against existing data and against other plausible interpretations of the data. Resulting decisions remain open to further scrutiny and reformulation.

Experiential learning theorists like Dewey and Jean Piaget maintain that learning is most effective when it begins with experience, in particular, experience that is problematic (Osterman & Kottkamp, 2004). Schön defined a problem as any "puzzling or troubling, or interesting phenomenon with which the individual is trying to deal" (Schön, 1983, p. 50). He suggested that such dilemmas practitioners face in the real world do not lend themselves to neat solutions. Instead, they require some improvising, inventing, and testing; that is, entering a reflective or inquiry cycle. A problem, defined as "a discrepancy between the present and the desired, or an intention and the actual impact", stimulates further inquiry, motivating a teacher to seek a deeper understanding of the situation at hand and to search for a better solution.

Regardless of the label, as uncertainty, dissonance, dilemma, problem, or conflict, some type of unsettling experience is a valuable stimulus to both cognitive growth as well as behavioral change. While experience is the starting point for learning, learning does not occur without reflection on experience. The old adage that experience is the greatest teacher tells only half the story. We actually learn only if we reflect on that experience.

PART II: KNOWLEDGE

DEFINING REFLECTIVE PRACTICE

Reflective teaching, **reflective thinking**, **reflective inquiry**, **reflection** and **reflective practice** are often used interchangeably, although there are slight distinctions (see Glossary). The term **reflective practice** is viewed here as the culmination of all other forms of reflection in that it is undertaken not solely to revisit the past but to guide future action.

Practice refers to one's repertoire of knowledge, attitudes, behaviors, and skills in specific areas of performance. For teachers, these areas include managing the classroom, designing instruction, establishing assessment strategies, and interacting with students, colleagues, and parents.

The following are some ways reflective practice has been described in the literature over the past two decades.

Reflective practice is:
- A dialogue of thinking and doing through which one becomes more skilled (Schön, 1987).
- A process that helps teachers think about what happened, why it happened, and what else could have been done to reach their goals (Cruickshank & Applegate, 1981).
- An inquiry approach that involves a personal commitment to continuous learning and improvement (York-Barr, Sommers, Ghere, & Montie, 2001).
- The practice of analyzing one's actions, decisions, or products by focusing on one's process for achieving them (Killion & Todnem, 1991).
- A critical, questioning orientation and a deep commitment to the discovery and analysis of information concerning the quality of a professional's designed action (Bright, 1996).
- A willingness to accept responsibility for one's professional practice (Ross, 1990).
- A systematic and comprehensive data-gathering process enriched by dialogue and collaborative effort (Osterman & Kottkamp, 2004).
- The use of higher-level thinking, such as critical inquiry and metacognition, which allow one to move beyond a

focus on isolated facts or data to perceive a broader context for understanding behavior and events (Hatton & Smith, 1995).
- The capacity to think creatively, imaginatively and, eventually, self-critically about classroom practice (Lasley, 1992).
- An ongoing process of examining and refining practice, variously focused on the personal, pedagogical, curricular, intellectual, societal, and/or ethical contexts associated with professional work (Cole & Knowles, 2000).

As you can see from these definitions, reflection goes much deeper than thinking about how to keep students quiet and on task.

Reflective Teachers Vs. Non-Reflective Teachers

Teachers who operate at a non-reflective level react without conscious consideration of alternative responses. Settling too quickly on only one explanation of a behavior or situation leads to a narrow range of potential solutions.

Non-reflective teachers react to individual classroom situations without connecting them to other events. Their orientation is reactive, attributing ownership of problems to students or others. They view student and classroom circumstances as beyond their control, seeing themselves as victims of circumstances. They are willing to take things for granted without questioning, justifying teaching methods without exploring alternatives. They enforce predetermined standards of operation without adapting or restructuring based on students' responses.

Reflective teachers spend a lot of time thinking about classroom interactions and consider both the intended as well as the unintended consequences of their actions. They engage in the thoughtful reconsideration of everything that happens in their classroom with an eye toward improvement. Non-reflective teachers often fail to recognize dilemmas, have little impetus for improvement, and are consequently unlikely to achieve their professional potential.

While all teachers make mistakes, what differentiates non-reflective from reflective teachers is that reflective teachers recognize, learn from, and strive to correct their mistakes.

ATTRIBUTES AND ATTITUDES OF REFLECTIVE PRACTITIONERS

For teachers to become reflective practitioners they must possess certain qualities or attributes and sustaining attitudes that are distinctly different from non-reflective practitioners.

Reflective Practitioners Take an Inquiry Stance

A primary distinction between reflective and non-reflective teachers is taking an **inquiry stance**. An inquiry stance is an active search for understanding. In an inquiry stance you shift your internal orientation from certainty to curiosity, and from arguing your position to exploring other positions. Teaching practice is in constant formation and is always open to further investigation. A tightly wrapped argument with your own conclusions doesn't encourage further unfolding of ideas or solutions. An inquiry stance helps teachers construct their own meaning and become partners in helping others do the same.

A Closer Look

TEN ATTRIBUTES OF A REFLECTIVE PRACTITIONER

- Reflects on and learns from experience
- Engages in ongoing inquiry
- Solicits feedback
- Remains open to alternative perspectives
- Assumes responsibility for own learning
- Takes action to align with new knowledge and understandings

- Observes self in the process of thinking
- Is committed to continuous improvement in practice
- Strives to align behaviors with values and beliefs
- Seeks to discover what is true

KEY ELEMENTS OF REFLECTIVE PRACTICE

- A deliberate pause, a purposeful slowing down, to allow for higher-level thinking processes

- An open-minded stance, recognizing there are many ways to view a particular circumstance, situation, or event

- A receptiveness to changing viewpoint and letting go of needing to be right

- A mindful state, being conscious of both thought and action

- An acknowledgment that doubt, perplexity, and tentativeness are part of the process

Three Essential Attitudes of Reflective Practitioners

The three essential attitudes or habits of mind first described by Dewey are still considered the foundation of reflective practice. They are: open-mindedness, responsibility, and wholeheartedness.

Open-mindedness

Open-mindedness is a willingness to consider new evidence as it occurs and to admit the possibility of error. Open-mindedness means being open to other points of view, appreciating that there are many ways to view a particular situation or event, and staying open to changing your own viewpoint. Part of open-mindedness is also letting go of needing to be right or wanting to win.

It requires hearing different views as valid ways of thinking, not as threats. Zeichner and Liston (1996) have described open-mindedness as "an active desire to listen to more sides than one, to give full attention to alternative possibilities, and to recognize the possibility of error even in our most dear beliefs."

Being open-minded requires the capacity to criticize oneself. Teachers who are unable to acknowledge their errors tend to blame their students for any problems that arise. For example, if 90% of the class fails a test, teachers who are open-minded consider the possibility that the material, method or approach was lacking, rather than accuse students of not studying.

Open-minded teachers continually seek new information that might challenge their taken-for-granted assumptions about teaching, thus enabling them to envision a broad range of potential solutions and making it more likely that dilemmas will be resolved.

Responsibility

Responsibility is the careful consideration of the consequences of one's actions, especially as they affect students. For Dewey, reflective thinking leads to responsible action. Responsibility refers to a teacher's willingness to examine all decision making (e.g., decisions about curriculum, instruction, evaluation, organization, management) from a coherent philosophical framework of teaching and learning.

Responsibility is the willingness to acknowledge that whatever one chooses to do will impact the lives of students in both foreseen and unforeseen ways. Demonstrating responsibility means owning the many positive and negative ways your actions might influence others, regardless of how things turn out.

Wholeheartedness

Dewey believed that when people are thoroughly interested in a cause, they throw themselves into it with a whole heart. Teachers who are wholehearted approach all situations with the attitude that they can learn something new. The "need-to-know" is the driving force for their learning. Farrell (2004) characterized **wholeheartedness** as "a commitment to seek every opportunity to learn."

Three Essential Practices for Becoming a Reflective Practitioner

While it's not possible to prescribe a step-by-step procedure, there are actions and practices that are fundamental to developing as a reflective practitioner. The following three practices are essential: 1) Solitary reflection, 2) Ongoing inquiry, and 3) Perpetual problem-solving. The first creates an opening for the possibility of reflection while the others allow for a way of developing teaching practice that accepts uncertainty, recognizes contextual bounds and considers multiple plausible explanations for events and circumstances.

Solitary Reflection

Making time for thoughtful consideration of your actions and critical inquiry into the impact of your own behavior keeps you alert to the consequences of your actions on students. It's important to engage in systematic reflection by making it an integral part of your daily practice. Keeping a reflective journal is one vehicle for ensuring time is set aside for daily reflection.

Teachers also need reflective time to consider the inevitable tradeoffs involved in everyday decisions that affect students. Any effort to become a reflective practitioner involves negotiating feelings of frustration and insecurity. Taking solitary time helps teachers come to accept that such feelings are a natural part of teaching.

Ongoing Inquiry

This practice involves unending questioning of the status quo and conventional wisdom by seeking your own truth. Being a fearless truth-seeker means examining the assumptions that underlie both classroom and school practices.

Perpetual Problem-solving

Perpetual problem-solvers are never satisfied that they have all the answers and constantly seek new information. Problems present opportunities to find better solutions, build relationships, and to teach students new coping strategies. Your *modus operandus* is solving problems, not enforcing preset standards of operation. The classroom serves as a laboratory for purposeful experimentation. A practice or procedure is never permanent. New insights, understandings and perspectives can bring previous decisions up for reevaluation at any time.

WANTED
A Reflective Practitioner

A person who is inherently curious; someone who doesn't have all the answers and isn't afraid to admit it; someone who is confident enough in his or her ability to accept challenges in a non-defensive manner; someone who is secure enough to make his or her thinking public and therefore subject to discussion; someone who is a good listener; someone who likes other people and trusts them to make the right decisions if given the opportunity; someone who is able to see things from another's perspective and is sensitive to the needs and feelings of others; someone who is able to relax and lean back and let others assume the responsibility of their own learning. Some experience desirable but not as important as the ability to learn from mistakes (Osterman & Kottkamp, 1993).

Activity Directions:

1. List all the qualities that are sought in this want ad.

2. Which ones do you possess?

3. Which one is your greatest strength?

4. Which one is your biggest challenge?

The following sections summarize various aspects that reflection entails so you can develop a better understanding of its role in teaching as well as in teacher development. Reflection is a complex and multifaceted term with many different dimensions.

Developing the Capacity to be Reflective

The aim of reflective practice is to think critically about oneself, one's assumptions, and one's teaching choices and actions (Cole & Knowles,

2000). Teachers who become reflective about their work come to know what they are doing, why they are doing it, and what will happen as a result of what they do. Whether focusing their reflection on subject matter, students' understanding, or the larger social context, teachers who develop as reflective practitioners understand and appreciate the complex realities of the classroom.

Focus and Goals of Reflective Practice

The focus of reflection can be at the level of examination of classroom practices and behaviors, goals and outcomes, or beliefs and values, manifested in expectations and assumptions. Teachers may reflect on the effects of a specific lesson or strategy, as well as on general practices, such as organizing the classroom, structuring the school day, establishing task structures and routines, interacting with students, and building relationships with both students and parents.

More in-depth reflection involves deliberations about one's aims and intentions, beliefs and values, as well as ethical dilemmas. Teachers may bring into question their goals, which encompass desired aims, outcomes, and intentions. They can be general such as creating the classroom as a learning community for students, or they can be more specific, such as assessing the impact of task structures like cooperative learning groups, buddy or peer groupings.

LEVELS OF REFLECTION

The term reflection is used to describe a vast array of practices. Just as with other popular terms, reflection can have a multitude of meanings as it is translated into professional teacher development. The literature describes numerous phases, levels, stages, types or dimensions of reflection. These descriptions range from mere thinking about a single aspect of a lesson to considering the ethical, social and political implications of teaching practice.

The various definitions evolving over several decades most commonly depict three levels of reflection (Day; 1993; Farrell, 2004; Handal & Lauvas, 1987; Jay & Johnson, 2002; Larrivee, 2004; Van Manen, 1977). In all of these descriptions of levels of reflection, critical reflection represents the zenith or ultimate aim.

The three levels are:

- An initial level focused on teaching functions, actions or skills, generally considering teaching episodes as isolated events.

- A more advanced level considering the theory and rationale for current practice.

- A higher order where teachers examine the ethical, social and political consequences of their teaching, grappling with the ultimate purposes of schooling.

Although there has been much discussion of the many different types and degrees of reflection, currently there is not any generally accepted terminology to define the various levels in the development of reflective practice. A point of deliberation is whether teachers should only reflect on behaviors and events within the confines of the classroom or whether they should also include the influence of the larger social and political contexts of the school community and the community at large.

The conceptual framework presented here represents a continuum of multiple levels adopting the terminology of surface reflection, pedagogical reflection, critical reflection and self-reflection.

Surface Reflection

At the first level, teachers' reflections focus on strategies and methods used to reach predetermined goals. They are concerned with what works in the classroom to keep students quiet and to maintain order, rather than with any consideration of the value of such goals as ends in themselves. At this level, the term technical has been most widely used (Van Manen, 1977). It has also been referred to as descriptive (Jay & Johnson, 2002). The term **surface reflection** is preferred by this author to depict a broader scope in this category, although still a low level of reflection.

Typical questions the teacher asks at the level of surface reflection are:

Did I spend too much time on groupwork today?

How can I keep students on-task?

Did I have enough (too many) activities?

How can I get students to pay better attention?

Pedagogical Reflection

At the next level, teachers reflect on educational goals, the theories underlying approaches, and the connections between theoretical principles and practice. This level has probably the least consensus in the literature as to its composition and label. It has been variously labeled practical, comparative, conceptual, contextual, theoretical, and deliberative. The term pedagogical is preferred by this author as a more inclusive term, merging all of the other concepts to connote a higher level of reflection based on application of teaching knowledge, theory and/or research.

Teachers engaging in **pedagogical reflection** strive to understand the theoretical basis for classroom practice and to foster consistency between espoused theory (what they say they do and believe) and theory-in-use (what they actually do in the classroom). Teachers reflecting at this level can determine when there is dissonance between what they practice and what they preach (e.g., seeing themselves as humanistic yet belittling students when they persist in disobeying rules).

Typical questions the teacher asks at the level of pedagogical reflection are:

How can I improve learning for all my students?

How can I build in better accountability for cooperative learning tasks?

Am I giving my students the opportunity to develop decision-making skills?

What else can I do to help students make connections to prior knowledge?

Is there a better way to accomplish this goal?

Teachers engaging in surface reflection, for example, may question how to limit the transition time between reading groups but may never question the larger issue of whether reading groups should exist (pedagogical reflection) or even if that structure limits the potential for some students with different cultural backgrounds (critical reflection).

Critical Reflection

At this next level, teachers reflect on the moral and ethical implications and consequences of classroom practices on students. They extend their considerations to issues beyond the classroom to include democratic ideals.

Acknowledging that classroom and school practices cannot be separated from the larger social and political realities, critically reflective teachers strive to become fully conscious of the range of consequences of their actions. Few teachers get through a day without facing ethical dilemmas. Even routine evaluative assessment of students' work is partly an ethical decision in that lack of opportunity to learn as well as impact on self-concept are ever-present considerations.

Although within the range of descriptions of reflective practice some incorporate a critical stance, many do not. Most typically, **critical reflection** is considered a higher-order level of reflection. Critical reflection adds the following dimensions:

- Questioning of underlying assumptions, biases, and values one brings to bear on their teaching.

- Conscious consideration of the ethical implications and consequences of practices on students and their learning.

- Examination of how instructional and other classroom practices contribute to social equity and to the establishment of a just society.

- Extended awareness beyond immediate instructional circumstances to include caring about democratic foundations and encouraging socially responsible actions.

The term critical reflection has the most consensus in the literature as a level of reflection examining the ethical, social and political consequences of one's teaching. Although even within this category there is considerable debate regarding the inclusion of self-reflection. Some definitions of critical reflection include the arena of self-reflection, also differentiated in the literature as *reflexive*, as distinguished from reflective. Some fail to acknowledge this category while others consider it to be imbedded in the category of critical reflection.

Typical questions the teacher asks at the level of critical reflection are:

Do all students in my class have daily opportunities to be successful?

Who is being included and who is being excluded in this classroom practice?

How might the ways I group students affect individual student's opportunity for success?

Does this classroom practice promote equity?

Do I have practices that differentially favor particular groups of students (e.g., males, females)?

Self-reflection

The conceptual models theorizing more than three levels generally single out the concept of **self-reflection** as a separate entity. Hatton and Smith (1995), Valli (1997), and York-Barr, Sommers, Ghere and Montie (2001) refer to this form of reflection as *dialogic, personalistic*, and *reflection-within*, respectively, highlighting the dimension of dialogue with oneself. However, the conceptualization of self-reflection presented here is a broader concept. Self-reflection focuses on examining how one's beliefs and values, expectations and assumptions, family imprinting, and cultural conditioning impact students and their learning (Larrivee, 2005). It is a process of search and discovery that uncovers the relationship of self to situation, of personal to professional. Based on the presumption that understanding oneself is a prerequisite condition to understanding others, self-reflection warrants distinction by itself.

The capacity for self-reflection is a distinguishing attribute of reflective practitioners. Self-reflection entails deep examination of **values** and **beliefs**, embodied in the assumptions teachers make and the expectations they have for students. Teacher behavior is driven by beliefs about students' capacity and willingness to learn, by assumptions about the behavior of students; especially those from different ethnic and social backgrounds, and by expectations formulated on the basis of the teacher's own value system.

Beliefs are convictions we hold dearly, having confidence in their truth, while acknowledging they are not susceptible to proof. They are enduring ideas about what is real.

Beliefs create the lens through which we view the world. Our beliefs shape our identity; hence shedding a dearly held belief shakes our very existence. For example, if a teacher tries to shed the belief that the teacher must be in total control to be effective, it means revealing uncertainty and vulnerability. A teacher's beliefs can be affirming or defeating, expansive or limiting.

Values are deeply held views about what we think is worthwhile. They steer how we behave on a daily basis and define the lines we will and will not cross. Values are our ideals; hence they are subjective and arouse an emotional response. In teaching, sets of values are often in conflict, challenging the teacher to weigh competing values against one another and play them off against the facts available. For example, a teacher may value being consistent while simultaneously valuing treating students justly. There are times when to be fair is to be inconsistent.

As teachers develop the capacity to be self-reflective, they become increasingly aware of how they are interactive participants in classroom encounters rather than innocent bystanders or victims. By developing the practice of self-reflection teachers learn to:

> (1) Slow down their thinking and reasoning process to become more aware of how they perceive and react to students
>
> (2) Bring to the surface some of their unconscious ways of responding to students.

Typical questions the teacher asks at the level of self-reflection are:

In what ways might I be modeling disrespect?

What is keeping me from trying to build a relationship with Pam?

Are there things I am doing that inhibit student self-management?

Why am I so intolerant of Adam's inappropriate behavior?

For teachers to continue to develop their professional work, they need to understand the formative as well as the continuing experiences and influences that have shaped and continue to shape their perspectives and practices.

Cole and Knowles (2000) distinguish between *reflective inquiry* and *reflexive inquiry*, describing the latter as tantamount to self-reflection as defined here. Underpinning reflective inquiry is the notion that assumptions behind all practice are subject to questioning. *Reflexive inquiry*, on the other hand, is reflective inquiry situated within the context of personal histories in order to make connections between personal lives and professional careers, and to understand personal (including early) influences on professional practice.

An example of progression from surface to self-reflection is depicted below.

A Closer Look — *Moving from Surface to Self-reflection*

Surface Reflection: *Are these good classroom rules for this group?*

Pedagogical Reflection: *Do my classroom rules represent reasonable expectations for my students?*

Critical Reflection: *Are the consequences for rule infractions just?*

Self-reflection: *Do I overreact when responding to Derrick's behavior because of my own biases?*

Teaching Practice Along the Reflective Continuum

Reflective practice is generally viewed as existing along a continuum. Although an individual teacher's progression is not necessarily linear, it is possible for teachers to reflect at different levels simultaneously or for various levels to be interwoven, depending on the topic of concern.

While each dimension of reflection can be useful in its own right as situations unfold, there is an implicit distinction in quality of reflection, with layers of quality moving from superficial to more significant to the potentially profound (Hatton & Smith, 1995; Hess, 1999; Jay & Johnson, 2002; Larrivee, 2004; McKenna, 1999; Smyth, 1989; Valli, 1997; Van Manen, 1977).

The increasing levels might also be characterized as falling along an "efficiency-value-worth continuum." At the first level the concern is mainly with means rather than ends. It entails selection and use of instructional methods primarily for their expediency. The second level adds questioning assumptions as well as consequences of particular strategies. Here teachers apply criteria to assess classroom practices to make individual and independent decisions about pedagogy. Teaching choices are based on a value commitment to a particular interpretive framework. The teacher analyzes and clarifies individual experiences, meanings, assumptions, and judgments for the purpose of making instructional decisions based on an interpretive understanding of what represents quality educational experiences. That is, decisions at the level of pedagogical reflection are based on a value judgment whereas decisions made at the level of critical reflection are based on a worth judgment. At the highest level of deliberation the worth of knowledge is in question. The teacher pursues worthwhile educational ends of self-determination based on the principles of justice, equality and freedom. This is what Van Manen (1977) referred to as the "classical politico-ethical meaning of social wisdom."

A Closer Look — Vignette for Reflection

While Ms. Dyer's class is working on story writing, she notices that Will is not working and is looking very frustrated. She asks him to brainstorm ideas for his story. He refuses, saying that he can't do it because he doesn't know how to spell.

Potential teacher's responses:
1. I would remind him that everyone is expected to be working. I would tell him to use the dictionary if he doesn't know how to spell the words. If he doesn't get started, I would tell him he can stay in for recess and do it then.

2. I would communicate that spelling is not important at this stage. What's important is to think of a story that the other students would enjoy reading. I would encourage him to use just the letters he hears for the words.

3. I would pair him with another student to work together.

4. I could allow him to dictate his ideas to me as I write them down.

5. Knowing that he has had little experience with the writing process, I would give further explanation of the brainstorming process as well as provide lots of modeling.

6. I could ask him to draw pictures to illustrate his thoughts and then dictate the

story into a tape recorder.

7. I would remind myself not to merely respond to his refusal and to try to understand what the message is behind his refusal. Then I would respond to both the content and the emotion behind his words.

8. Because he has had some negative experiences with writing, making him apprehensive about putting his thoughts down on paper, I would try to build his confidence. I would make sure I provided a great deal of encouragement for every effort he makes.

Activity Directions:
For each of the identified options, note if you think it indicates reflective thinking. Then try to categorize the level of reflection evident in the teacher's response.

REFLECTION DIRECTION

While Schön (1983) initially made the distinction between *reflection-in-action* and *reflection-on-action*, Killion and Todnem (1991) added the concept of *reflection-for-action*, connoting a deliberate intent to change. York-Barr, Sommers, Ghere, and Montie (2001) used the terminology of reflection direction and added the concept of *reflection-within* depicting four different directions that can guide reflection. One can reflect in the present (in), reflect back (on), reflect forward (for action) or reflect within as described below.

Reflection-in-action is observing thinking and action as they are occurring for the purpose of making immediate adjustments as classroom events unfold. Here a reevaluation occurs on the spot. New data are linked to what is already known allowing the teacher to adapt in the moment. It is often difficult to reflect while events are occurring, but when it is possible, it is a very powerful type of reflection. Keen awareness of what is going on in the present allows the teacher to make adjustments while in the process of teaching or responding. It requires a high level of consciousness. With this type of reflection, for example, the teacher may notice that engagement is trailing off and will do something novel to regain students' attention. As Schön noted, this form of reflection is often tacit.

Reflection-on-action is looking back on and learning from experience or action in order to affect future action. Often reflection during, or simultaneous with, actions is difficult because of the multiple demands teachers have to juggle in the classroom. For instance, focusing attention on completing a lesson may distract from paying attention to the way in which the teacher interacts with students. Hence, reflection often requires a perspective of a meta-position, a looking back after the action has taken place. Van Manen (1991) referred to this as *recollective reflection* noting that it promotes deeper insight into past experiences. Reflecting after being removed from an event is probably the most frequently used form of reflection given that it may be too challenging to reflect while engaged in the teaching process with so many things vying for the teacher's simultaneous attention.

Reflection-for-action is analyzing behavior with the designated purpose of taking some action to change. What differentiates this type of reflection is that it is proactive in nature. Killion and Todnem contend that it is the desired outcome of both *reflection-in-action* and *reflection-on-action*. They make the case that reflection is not so much for the purpose of revisiting the past or becoming aware of our metacognitive processes, but to guide future action. Farrell (2004) noted that teachers can not only use this type of reflection to prepare for the future by using knowledge from what happened during class and what they reflected on after class, but also as a means of detecting inconsistencies between beliefs and practice.

Teachers use this type of reflection when they already recognize that they need to change something, such as a relationship with a student, or a task structure to enhance participation. Here the teacher entertains specific actions or interventions with students, the learning environment, or school community that are likely to produce more desirable results. The systematic investigation on classroom practices conducted via **action research** also falls into the category of reflection-for-action.

Teachers using reflection-for-action are able to move out of focusing on their dissatisfaction with what is happening now to concentrate on closing the discrepancy between the current situation and what they would like to see. By focusing on their vision for the preferred future they put their energy into closing the gap between what is and what might be.

Reflection-within is inquiring about personal purposes, intentions, and feelings. In this form of reflection, teachers might question what is preventing them from taking action or keeping their perspective limited. As such, this concept is very similar to self-reflection as defined earlier.

Here teachers may ask themselves questions like the following.

What were my intentions when I did that?

What triggered such an emotionally charged response?

Am I considering alternative explanations for what happened with Maria?

4-STEP PROCESS FOR GUIDING REFLECTION

The following process can guide reflection-on-action and reflection-for-action (York-Barr, Sommers, Ghere, & Montie, 2001). It moves through the sequence of asking what? why? so what? and now what?

A Closer Look	*Guided Reflection on a Significant Event*

Think about a significant event or interaction that occurred in your classroom that was unsettling or challenging. Consider the following questions to prompt your reflection about the experience.
1. What happened?
2. Why do I think things happened that way?
3. So what?
   Why was this significant to me?
   What have I learned?
   What questions remain?
4. Now what?
   What are the implications for action?

PART III: APPLICATIONS

THE CAPACITY TO REFRAME: A CRUCIAL ATTRIBUTE OF REFLECTIVE PRACTITIONERS

When faced with a problem, teachers basically have two choices--change the situation or change their reaction to the situation. Often teachers can't change the situation, but they can change how they respond by learning to **reframe** or reposition classroom situations and school circumstances. Reframing means putting the experience in a new frame, one that views the situation from a different angle or one that includes parts of the picture that weren't visible from the first vantage point.

The term **reposition** connotes the idea of changing your perception by moving out of your old position and creating a new position from which to view a situation (Larrivee, 1996). It involves developing the capacity to look at what's happening, withholding judgment, while simultaneously recognizing that the meaning you attribute to it is no more than your interpretation filtered through your cumulative experience.

Breaking through familiar cycles necessitates a shift in ways of thinking, perceiving and interpreting classroom events. When a student acts out, one teacher sees a personal attack while another sees a cry for help. It is the teacher's interpretation of the student's behavior, or the meaning attached to the behavior, that determines how the teacher will respond. It's a teacher's personal framing that shapes how he or she attributes meaning to classroom experiences.

Seeing new ways of interpreting a situation enables a teacher to move beyond a limited perspective and assign new meaning to the classroom situations encountered. By repositioning a seemingly negative event, the teacher seizes the opportunity to discover the potential in a situation.

A Closer Look — *Repositioning Events and Situations*

Some helpful ways of repositioning in the classroom include:
- Repositioning confrontation as energy to be rechanneled
- Repositioning an attack as a cry for help
- Repositioning conflict as opportunity for relationship building
- Repositioning defiance as a request for communication

- Repositioning attention-seeking as a plea for recognition

Challenging Underlying Beliefs and Creating Dissonance

Teachers who develop as reflective practitioners continually challenge the underlying beliefs that drive their present behavior. However, the channel to changing beliefs is not direct; it is through critically examining assumptions, interpretations and expectations.

Questioning assumptions, naming issues, and confronting limiting beliefs is an emotional experience. Examining efficacy, value and worth of classroom practices necessarily creates tension. Promoting tension, uncertainty, and dissonance helps to unveil the multiple dimensions of dilemmas and consequently reveal a wider range of options. Reflecting on teaching practices can at times be discouraging and defeating, as well as empowering and exhilarating. Out of the conflict and discomfort can come invaluable learning and insight.

AVENUES TO DEVELOPING REFLECTIVE PRACTICE

To develop the habits of mind necessary to become reflective practitioners, preservice and novice teachers often need to be explicitly prompted to think, respond, and act in new ways. Reflection is enhanced when mentoring or coaching is provided that allows teachers as learners to tap into their own realm of experiences, reflect on those experiences, and construct personal meaning to inform their developing practice. Reflection, especially critical reflection and self-reflection, are complex constructs requiring strategically constructed mediation or facilitation.

Much of the literature grapples with moving beyond the surface level of reflection to engage in pedagogical reflection and critical reflection. According to the research conducted by Hatton and Smith (1995) with teachers in preservice training, teacher progression through various levels of reflection appears to be developmental in the sense that the technical level represents a useful starting point for addressing concerns. For example, they noted that teachers may need to reflect first on areas of technical skill before being able to compare different teaching strategies and weigh their relative merit.

Other researchers have identified processes that can help preservice and novice teachers move along the reflection continuum. The generally accepted position is that these teachers can be helped to reflect at higher levels with carefully constructed guidance (e.g., Putorak, 1993, 1996; Rudney & Guillaume, 1990; Wildman & Niles, 1987; Yost, Sentner, & Forlanza-Bailey, 2000). Collier (1999) noted that establishing self-monitoring and self-reflective activities early on can promote the kind of self-awareness that allows preservice teachers to hear and listen to their own voices. Focusing on what they already know and believe about teaching has proven to be a useful starting point (Wideen, Meyer-Smith, & Moon, 1998).

Some mediated structures and other vehicles that have been found to be useful in promoting reflection include journal writing, teacher narratives, autobiography, metaphor, critical incidents, support groups, critical friends, and action research. Merging these task structures in creative ways and utilizing them individually, collaboratively, and with facilitated coaching is likely to have the greatest potential for promoting higher-order reflection.

Journal Writing (open, reflective, interactive, and dialogue)

The act of maintaining and reviewing a journal over time can serve as a useful tool for reflection. Having a record of thoughts, feelings, issues and concerns can provide both a window of the past and a gateway to the future.

Practical Tips and Strategies	*Journal Writing for Reflection*

Journal writing can serve as a tool for:
- Looking more objectively at classroom behaviors
- Naming issues and posing questions
- Recording critical incidents
- Identifying cause and effect relationships

- Discovering habits of thought and behavior
- Working through internal conflicts
- Seeing patterns of unsuccessful strategies over time
- Tracing life themes

Journal writing as a systematic self-reflection process enables teachers to recognize their contribution to the experiences they encounter in the classroom. Making regular journal entries can help teachers become more aware of what is going on in both their inner and outer worlds. Journal writing also develops self-discipline.

Journal writing can be used in a number of ways to encourage reflection (Calderhead, 1991; Collier, 1999; Dobbins, 1996; Keating, 1993; Ross, 1990; Smyth, 1992; Surbeck, Han, & Moyer; Wiltz, 1999; Yost, 1997; Yost, Forlanza-Bailey, & Shaw, 1999). Reflection can be facilitated via guided prompts, structuring periodic rereading of previous entries to search for any emerging patterns, and posing questions in a nonjudgmental way as a means of creating ongoing dialogue.

One significant finding from Dobbins' (1996) research using journal writing with preservice teachers was that being specifically prompted to focus on their own learning produced reflections with a deeper focus in which they were able to confront broader educational issues in the process of clarifying their own beliefs. Similarly, there is evidence that when preservice teachers are engaged in journal writing over time they develop the habit of reflection (Yost, 1997, Yost, Forlanza-Bailey, & Shaw, 1999).

Dialogue journals, also referred to as interactive journals, are first individually written and then shared with another person who makes inquiries for the purpose of expanding thinking (Keating, 1993). That person might be an instructor, mentor, peer coach or critical friend.

Autobiographical journal writing coupled with deliberate questioning prompts can stimulate greater awareness of personal values and implicit theories of teaching (Ross, 1990). The regular feedback from a mentor serving in a coaching role can be a valuable tool to move teacher trainees along the reflection continuum.

Smyth (1991) found posing a series of four questions, respectively moving from description to meaning to confrontation to reconstruction, to be a powerful tool for prompting higher-order reflection. The questions are:

(1) What do I do?	*Description*
(2) What does it mean?	*Meaning*
(3) How did I come to be like this?	*Confrontation*
(4) How might I do things differently?	*Reconstruction*

Teacher Narratives (autobiography, metaphor, case story writing)

Narratives other than journal writing can render a rich understanding of what takes place in the minds of developing teachers as they construct their reality of teaching. **Teacher narratives** are stories written by and about teachers and can be used as the source of narrative inquiry (Cole & Knowles, 2000; Sparks-Langer & Colton, 1991; Zeichner, 1983). It is a more disciplined from of writing than journaling in that it has a structure and a focus, the intent to communicate a story. Either keen observers or teachers themselves write real stories about teaching that illuminate the realities, dilemmas and rewards of teaching. Reflecting on teacher narratives can yield insights about motivations for teacher actions, the complexities of teaching, and about teachers themselves (Sparks-Langer & Colton, 1991; Taggart & Wilson, 1998). Teacher narratives can also be specifically designed to be used as case studies with the explicit purpose of reflecting on a specific problem. Using a vehicle of case story writing based on student teaching experiences, Hunter and Hatton (1998) found that combined peer and instructor collaboration helped preservice teachers move toward critical reflection.

Autobiographical sketches, also called personal histories, are a specialized form of teacher narratives (Sparks-Langer & Colton, 1994). These stories of a more personal and in-depth nature offer insight into the past to uncover preconceived theories of practice. When teachers write about their own biographies and how they think these have shaped the construction of their values, then they are able to see more clearly how social and institutional forces beyond the classroom and school have had an influence.

Johnson (1994) and Lasley (1992) advocated the use of **metaphors** to help teachers become aware of their teaching identities and develop alternative ways to think about an issue. Marshall (1990) contends that the reflection that occurs in the examination of personal teaching metaphors involves reframing the lens through which a teacher perceives a problem. According to Schön, this is a critical attribute of reflective practitioners.

Metaphors bear the images teachers have of themselves as teachers, their professional identity (Bullough, Knowles, & Crow, 1992). The practical theories of teachers are often expressed as metaphors as opposed to the more logical forms of expression. They often appear in the natural language teachers use to talk about their teaching (Munby & Russell, 1990). The knowledge-in-action embedded in the practical theories of teachers often cannot be adequately depicted in their statements of knowledge; hence metaphor can be a way to bridge the known to the new.

Through metaphors teachers can elaborate and turn abstractions into real images, helping to give them firmer handles on slippery concepts such as teaching.

The following metaphors written by beginning teachers offer a glimpse of the images teachers have of themselves as teachers:

A teacher is like a song creating memories and bringing comfort when you hear it.

A teacher is like a caterpillar because you are continually stretching out then pulling back. It's pretty stressful if you try to be stretched out all the time, so you have to remember to pull back. But if you always pull back you go nowhere.

Critical Incident

Though generally conceived as a self-generated incident, a **critical incident** could also be a carefully chosen real-world example or case study of a teaching dilemma intended to serve as a springboard for reflection. Examining a critical incident can be a tool for deepening the level of reflection. Pultorak (1996) found that writing about critical incidents or dilemmas rather than typical daily events promoted critical reflection in novice teachers. Likewise, Griffin (2003) found that using critical incidents with explicit prompts and coaching increased the capacity of preservice teachers to engage in higher order reflection.

Descriptions of high and low moments in their practice, or details of significant incidents that stand out in their lives as teachers, provide the impetus to grapple with problems and dilemmas becoming the basis for critical investigation. By sharing critical incident responses, teachers come to realize that their individual stories have generic qualities and themes embedded within them. They discover that their personal struggles are not so different from those experienced by their colleagues. What they thought were idiosyncratic failings or inadequacies come to be seen as common experiences.

A Closer Look	*Critical Incident: Low Points of Practice*

Thinking back over the past few months, identify an incident that caused you the greatest distress in your teaching, one that may have kept you awake at night thinking about what you should have done. Write about where and when it happened, who was involved, and what it was about the incident that was so distressing to you.

Support Groups and Critical Friends

Teaching is a complex and personal expression of multiple and varied forms of knowledge and knowing. Much of what teachers do is implicit, hidden from the practitioner but observable by others. An individual teacher's thinking needs to be confirmed, modified, or stimulated to deeper levels of understanding by reflecting aloud.

A major purpose of reflective practice is to test for the presence of assumptions and biases in the information one accesses. The checks and balances of peers' and critical friends' perspectives can help beginning teachers recognize when they may be devaluing information or using self-confirming reasoning, weighing evidence with a predisposition to confirm a theory rather than consider alternative theories that are equally plausible.

Reflective practice involves teachers questioning the goals, values, and assumptions that guide their work, entailing critical questions about the means, ends, and contexts of teaching. Engaging in such questioning can best occur in a supportive learning community, such as that provided in **support groups** or **critical friends**.

Such support can help teachers keep from getting stuck in destructive habits to deal with the stress of teaching and provide a buffer against the inevitable low points enroute to becoming a reflective practitioner

(Brookfield, 1995). Ideally, a support group or critical friend provides a safe haven to be vulnerable, admit mistakes and ask for help.

Their function is not only to empathize with others' dilemmas but also to point out incongruencies in practice and fallacies in thinking. It often takes others to mirror back experiences and perceptions to open up a new way of seeing things.

It is important to build a support system to provide comfort and compassion as well as understanding, direction, and when necessary, redirection. Recurring problems can erode self-perceptions of ability to find adequate solutions to problems that plague teachers on a day-to-day basis, leading to a preoccupation with the negative aspects of teaching. Collaborative peer support is one vehicle for supplanting such negative attitudes and self-appraisals with encouragement.

Peer conversation helps to break down the isolation many teachers feel. Colleagues' perceptions help teachers realize the commonality of their individual experiences. There is often much more that unites them than they realize. Collaborative dialogue helps teachers become aware of how much they take for granted in their own teaching and how much of their practice is judgmental.

ACTION RESEARCH

One of the most widely recognized ways to reflect on and improve practice is action research (Carr & Kemmis, 1986; Cochran-Smith & Lyle, 1993; Cole & Knowles, 2000; Dana & Yendol-Silva, 2003; Glanz, 1998; McFee, 1993; Osterman & Kottkamp, 2004). It is a systematic inquiry process conducted by and for those taking the action. Teachers assume the role of researcher in their own classrooms as part of a professional reflective stance.

Action research is a form of disciplined inquiry ranging from simply raising a question about some educational practice and collecting information to answer the question, to doing statistical analyses to determine whether test results from an experimental group are statistically significant. The process is similar to other reflection frameworks with the primary distinguishing feature being the emphasis on formalizing research questions and then collecting and analyzing data to take informed action.

The purpose and intent of action research is not the development of universal principles to be applied to all teaching situations. Rather, each classroom is envisioned as a small culture created by teacher and students as they work together over a period of time. The ultimate intent of action research based on this view of teaching is to build and verify a coherent explanation of how a particular classroom works.

A Closer Look — *Reflecting About a Teaching Practice*

Mr. Bates was nearing the end of his first year of teaching fifth grade in an urban district. He wanted students to work together in his classroom and he believed that when students learned together they could all benefit. During the year, he had tried a variety of ways to gather his students into cooperative learning groups, but none got him the results he wanted. He needed to find more effective ways to organize for cooperative learning. He decided to conduct his own action research.

He learned from reading the research on collaborative learning that he needed to accomplish the following to be successful:

(1) Plan the groupwork to specifically align with the particular learning goals of the lesson.
(2) Provide a structure for the kind of social interaction he wanted to see among group members.
(3) Identify what kinds of group talk would serve as evidence that learning was being achieved during the group sessions.
(4) Exercise caution when entering the group setting not to disturb the dynamics already in place.

Mr. Bates realized that he had to be much more strategic in structuring the groups to accomplish the learning goals he had for his students. Adhering to these four guidelines, he changed the way he approached and structured group time with his class. He also made a plan to collect data to make sure these changes promoted the kind of collaborative climate he wanted.

Activity Directions:
1. Describe a situation you have had similar to Mr. Bates' where new information or research caused you to make a significant change in a teaching practice.

2. What information, knowledge, or research findings would you like to have about a teaching method you are currently using or would like to use?

3. What is an area of your teaching that you would like to see working better? What would you like to see that's not happening now?

PART IV: EXTENSIONS

BOOKS

Brookfield, S. D. (1995). *Becoming a critically reflective teacher*. San Francisco, CA: Jossey-Bass.

Farrell, T. S. (2004). *Reflective practice in action: 80 reflective breaks for busy teachers*. Thousand Oaks, CA: Corwin Press.

Jay, J. K. (2003). *Quality teaching: Reflection as the heart of practice*. Lanham, MD: Scarecrow Press.

Larrivee, B. (2005). *Authentic classroom management: Creating a learning community and building reflective practice*. Boston, MA: Allyn & Bacon.

Osterman, K. P., & Kottkamp, R. B. (2004). *Reflective practice for educators: Improving schooling through professional development*. Thousand Oaks, CA: Corwin Press.

York-Barr, J., Sommers, W. A., Ghere, G. S., & Montie, J. (2001). *Reflective practice to improve schools*. Thousand Oaks, CA: Corwin Press.

Zeichner, K. M., & Liston, D. P. (1996). *Reflective teaching: An introduction*. Mahwah, NJ: Lawrence Erlbaum.

GLOSSARY

action research Any systematic inquiry conducted by teacher researchers or other stakeholders in the teaching/learning environment to gather information about how their particular schools operate, how they teach, and how well their students learn.

beliefs The conclusions we draw over time about our experiences that significantly influence our ways of thinking and behaving.

critical friends Both support and challenge each other to look critically at their classroom practices.

critical incident A vividly remembered event which is unanticipated and has significant implications related to your teaching.

critical reflection The conscious consideration of the moral and ethical implications and consequences of classroom practices on students.

inquiry stance A learning stance in which you actively search for understanding.

metaphor A way of illuminating features through comparison to understand and experience one kind of thing in terms of another.

open-mindedness Listening to other points of view, considering alternatives, and acknowledging our own potential for error.

pedagogical reflection At this level, reflection is guided by a conceptual framework and beliefs about teaching are grounded in theory or research.

reflective teaching Approaching teaching as a cyclical process in which teachers continually monitor, evaluate and revise their own practice.

reflective thinking Involves developing the attitudes of open-mindedness, responsibility, and wholeheartedness.

reflection-for-action Proactive thinking in order to guide future action.

reflection-in-action Thinking about events in the classroom as they happen to make immediate adjustments.

reflection-on-action Thinking back on what was done to gain deeper insight.

reflection-within Inquiring about personal purposes, intentions, and feelings.

reflective inquiry A systematic and disciplined approach to understanding problems, finding and implementing solutions, and assessing their results.

reflective practice A questioning orientation toward one's actions, decisions, and outcomes and an acceptance of responsibility for one's professional practice.

reflective practitioners Those who perpetually consider alternatives, taking action to continually improve practice throughout their professional career.

reframe To put an experience in a new frame, one that views the situation from a different angle or includes parts of the picture that weren't visible from the first vantage point.

reposition To change your perception by moving out of a limited perspective to see new ways of interpreting a situation.

responsibility Taking ownership for the consequences of your actions and their impact on students.

self-reflection Examining how one's beliefs and values, expectations and assumptions, family imprinting, and cultural conditioning impact students and their learning.

support groups Can be either informal or formal groups of peers who meet on a regular basis to provide an opportunity for communication, reflection, and socialization.

surface reflection At this level of reflection, the teacher's examination of teaching methods is confined to tactical issues concerning how best to achieve predefined objectives and standards.

teacher narratives Stories written by and about teachers that can be used as the source of inquiry.

values Deeply-held views about what we think is worthwhile.

wholeheartedness Thoroughly committing yourself to seeking better solutions to perplexing concerns.

REFERENCES

Bright, B. (1996). Reflecting on "reflective practice." *Studies in the Education of Adults, 28*(2), 162-184.

Brookfield, S. D. (1995). *Becoming a critically reflective teacher.* San Francisco, CA: Jossey-Bass.

Bullough, R., Knowles, J. G., & Crow, N. (1992). *Emerging as a teacher.* London: Routledge.

Calderhead, J. (1991). The nature and growth of knowledge in student teaching. *Teaching and Teacher Education, 8* (5/6), 531-535.

Carr, W., & Kemmis, S. (1986). *Becoming critical: Education, knowledge and action research.* London: Falmer.

Cochran-Smith, M., & Lytle, S. (1993). *Inside/Outside: Teacher research and knowledge.* New York: Teachers College Press.

Cole, A. L., & Knowles, J. G. (2000). *Researching teaching: Exploring teacher development through reflective inquiry.* Boston: Allyn and Bacon.

Collier, S. T. (1999). Characteristics of reflective thought during the student teaching experience. *Journal of Teacher Education, 50*(3), 173-181.

Cruickshank, D., & Applegate, J. (1981). Reflective teaching as a strategy for teacher growth: *Educational Leadership, 38*(7), 553-554.

Dana, N. F., & Yendol-Silva, D. (2003). *The reflective educator's guide to classroom research.* Thousand Oaks, CA: Corwin Press.

Day, C. (1993). Reflection: a necessary but not sufficient condition for professional development. *British Educational Research Journal, 19*, 83-93.

Dewey, J. (1910/1933). *How we think: A restatement of the relation of reflective thinking to the educative process.* Lexington, MA: Heath.

Dewey, J. (1938). *Logic: The theory of inquiry.* Troy, MO: Holt, Rinehart & Winston.

Dobbins, R., (1996). The challenge of developing a 'reflective practicum.' *Asia-Pacific Journal of Teacher Education, 24*(3), 269-280.

Farrell, T. S. (2004). *Reflective practice in action: 80 reflective breaks for busy teachers.* Thousand Oaks, CA: Corwin Press.

Glanz, J. (1998). *Action research: An educational leader's guide to school improvement.* Norwood, MA: Christopher-Gordon.

Griffin, M. L. (2003). Using critical incidents to promote and assess reflective thinking in preservice teachers. *Reflective Practice, 4(2),* 207-220.

Handal, G., & Lauvas, P. (1987). *Promoting reflective teaching.* Milton Keynes, UK: Open University Press.

Hatton, N., & Smith, D. (1995). Reflection in teacher education: Towards definition and implementation. *Teaching and Teacher Education, 11*(1), 22-49.

Hess, D. (1999). *Developing a typology for teaching preservice students to reflect: A case of curriculum deliberation.* Paper presented at the annual meeting of the American Educational Research Association, Montreal.

Hunter, J. & Hatton, N. (1998). Approaches to the writing of cases: Experience with preservice master of education students. *Asia-Pacific Journal of Teacher Education, 26,* 235-246.

Jay, J. K. (2003). *Quality teaching: Reflection as the heart of practice.* Lanham, MD: Scarecrow Press.

Jay, J. K., & Johnson, K. L. (2002). Capturing complexity: A typology of reflective practice for teacher education. *Teaching and Teacher Education, 18*, 73-85.

Johnston, M. (1994). Contrasts and similarities in case studies of teacher reflection and change. *Curriculum Inquiry, 24*(1), 9-26.

Keating, C. N. (1993). Promoting growth through dialogue journals. In G. Wells (Ed.), *Changing schools from within: Creating communities of inquiry* (pp. 217-236). Toronto, Canada: Ontario Institute for Studies in Education Press.

Kesley, J. G. (1993). Learning from teaching: Problems, problem-formulation and the enhancement of problem-solving capability. In P. Hallinger, K. A., Leithwood, & J. Murphy (Eds.), *A cognitive perspective on educational administration* (pp. 231-252). New York: Teachers College Press.

Killion, J., & Todnem, G. (1991). A process of personal theory building. *Educational Leadership, 48*(6), 14-17.

King, P. M., & Kitchener, K. S. (1994). *Developing reflective judgment.* San Francisco, CA: Jossey-Bass.

Larrivee, B. (1996). *Moving into balance.* Santa Monica, CA: Shoreline.

Larrivee, B. (2000). Transforming teaching practice: Becoming the critically reflective teacher. *Reflective Practice, 1*(3), 293-307.

Larrivee, B. (2004). *Assessing teachers' level of reflective practice as a tool for change.* Paper presented at the Third International Conference on Reflective Practice, Gloucester, UK.

Larrivee, B. (2005). *Authentic classroom management: Creating a learning community and building reflective practice.* Boston, MA: Allyn & Bacon.

Lasley, T. J. (1992). Inquiry and reflection: Promoting teacher reflection. *Journal of Staff Development, 13*(1), 24-29.

Marshall, H. (1990). Metaphor as an instructional tool in encouraging student teacher reflection. *Theory into Practice, 29*(2), 128-132.

McFee, G. (1993). Reflections on the nature of action research. *Cambridge Journal of Education, 23*(2), 173-183.

McKenna, H. (1999). *A pedagogy of reflection: Pathfinding in times of change.* Paper presented at the annual conference of the American Association of Colleges of Teacher Education, Washington, D.C.

Munby, H., & Russell, T. (1990). Metaphor in the study of teachers' professional knowledge. *Theory into Practice, 29*(2), 116-121.

Osterman, K. P., & Kottkamp, R. B. (1993/2004). *Reflective practice for educators: Improving schooling through professional development.* Thousand Oaks, CA: Corwin Press.

Pultorak, E. G. (1993). Facilitating reflective thought in novice teachers. *Journal of Teacher Education, 44,* 288-295.

Pultorak, E. G. (1996). Following the developmental process of reflection in novice teacher: Three years of investigation. *Journal of Teacher Education, 47,* 283-291.

Ross, D. D. (1990). Programmatic structures for the preparation of reflective teachers. In R. T. Clift, W. R. Houston, & M. C. Pugach (Eds.), *Encouraging reflective practice in education: An analysis of issues and programs* (pp. 97-118). New York: Teachers College Press.

Rudney, G., & Guillaume, A. (1990). Reflective teaching for student teachers. *The Teacher Educator, 25*(3), 13-20.

Schön, D. A. (1983). *The reflective practitioner: How professionals think in action.* New York: Basic Books.

Schön, D. A. (1987). *Educating the reflective practitioner.* San Francisco: Jossey-Bass.

Smyth, J. (1989). Developing and sustaining critical reflection in teacher education. *Journal of Teacher Education, 40*(2), 2-9.

Smyth, J. (1991). *Teachers as collaborative learners.* Milton Keynes Open University Press.

Smyth, J. (1992). Teacher's work and the politics of reflection. *American Education Research Journal, 29*(2), 267-300.

Sparks-Langer, G., & Colton, A. (1991). Synthesis of research on teachers' reflective thinking. *Educational Leadership, 48(6),* 37-44.

Sparks-Langer, G., & Colton, A. (1994). Reflective decision making: The cornerstone of school reform. *Journal of Staff Development, 15*(1), 2-7.

Surbeck, E., Han, E., & Moyer, J. (1991). Assessing reflective responses in journals. *Educational Leadership, 48*(6), 25-27.

Taggart, G., & Wilson, A. P. (1998). *Promoting reflective thinking in teachers.* Thousand Oaks, CA: Corwin Press.

Valli, L. (1997). Listening to other voices: A description of teacher reflection in the United States. *Peabody Journal of Education, 72*(1), 67-88.

Van Manen, M. (1977). Linking ways of knowing with ways of being practical. *Curriculum Inquiry, 6*(3), 205-228.

Van Manen, M. (1991). Reflectivity and pedagogical moment: The normativity of pedagogical thinking and acting. *Journal of Curriculum Studies, 23*, 507-536.

Wideen, M., Mayer-Smith, J., & Moon, B. (1998). A critical analysis of the research on learning to teach: Making the case for an ecological perspective on inquiry. *Review of Educational Research, 68*(2), 130-178.

Wildman, T. M. & Niles, J. A. (1987). Reflective teachers: Tensions between abstractions and realities. *Journal of Teacher Education, 38*(4), 25-31.

York-Barr, J., Sommers, W. A., Ghere, G. S., & Montie, J. (2001). *Reflective practice to improve schools*. Thousand Oaks, CA: Corwin Press.

Yost, D. S., Sentner, S. M., & Forlenza-Bailey, A. (2000). An examination of the construct of critical reflection: Implications for teacher education programming in the 21st century. *Journal of Teacher Education, 51*(1), 39-48.

Yost, D. S. (1997). The moral dimensions of teaching and preservice teachers: Can moral dispositions be influenced? *Journal of Teacher Education, 48,* 281-292.

Yost, D. S., Forlenza-Bailey, A., & Shaw, S. F. (1999). The teachers who embrace diversity: The role of reflection, discourse, and field experience in education. *The Professional Educator, 21*(2), *1-14*.

Zeichner, K. M. (1983). Alternative paradigms of teacher education. *Journal of Teacher Education, 39*(3), 3-9.

Zeichner, K. M., & Liston, D. P. (1996). *Reflective teaching: An introduction*. Mahwah, NJ: Lawrence Erlbaum